New Mags City Guide
Paris

For years, I've traveled the world as a design and lifestyle expert. Every time I discover an inspiring place, I make a note of it. Over time, this list has grown to include many outstanding destinations. People often ask me for travel recommendations. Obviously, most people don't have the time to find the best spots, because it requires time, and time is a scarce resource for many. That's why we created this series of city guides. Not just any collection of guides, but the best, most beautiful, and most practical, presented as a real book. I believe the ideal city guide is tangible, something you can bring along on your journey, especially handy when your smartphone runs out of battery.

Special thanks to Jesper Svangaard from New Mags for his enthusiasm and publishing expertise, and to Mario Depicolzuane, our art director, whose studio's design brought this guide to life. I'm also deeply grateful to all the incredible locations featured and to everyone who helped bring this project to life.

We hope that you, as a reader, will embrace our city guide and find it valuable on your travels. After all, that's the true purpose of this book.

BIGBUS PARIS

Paris is perhaps the most beautiful city in Europe, with its grand monuments, stunning architecture, wide boulevards, and charming neighbourhoods. It has everything the heart desires. It's a city that holds on to its traditions. People cherish their cafés, small specialty shops, boulangeries, and bistros serving classic French cuisine. Of course, you'll find trendy coffee shops, natural wine bars, and neo-bistros offering a modern take on French food and culture, but Paris still insists on preserving its rich history and traditions. And I love both. Fashion is everywhere. As one of the three fashion

capitals alongside London and Milan, it lives and breathes style. From high-street brands to haute couture, from streetwear and vintage fashion to timeless Parisian elegance, the city embodies it all. Every year, millions of tourists flock to the city to see the Louvre, Notre Dame, the Eiffel Tower, the Arc de Triomphe, and countless other sights. But thankfully, Paris is so much more, and that is exactly what this guide is about. A selection of my favourite places. Far from all of them, there wouldn't be enough pages, but some of the very best, spread across my favourite districts.

Salle au 3ème
ODETTE
Salle au 1er
ODETTE
Les meilleurs choux à la crème de Paris
Patisserie
ODETTE
PARIS
RUE
GALANDE

Élysée Montmartre
Hôtel Amour
Hôtel Grand Amour
Grand Pigalle Experimental
L'Eldorado
Hôtel des Académies et des Arts
Le Grand Hôtel Cayré
Hotel Piscine Molitor
Le Pigalle
The Hoxton Paris

Stay

Élysée Montmartre

78 Blvd Marguerite de Rochechouart, 75018 Paris

@em.hotel
emhotel.fr
+33 183 751585

On the border between the vibrant Pigalle and the bohemian Montmartre lies a hotel that redefines luxury. Here, luxury isn't about excess, it's about the rare opportunity to immerse yourself in a world shaped by art, music, and history.

Until the late 1980s, this building partially served as the artist dressing rooms for the Élysée Montmartre concert hall. This iconic venue of Parisian culture has hosted legendary artists such as David Bowie, Daft Punk, Red Hot Chili Peppers, Beastie Boys, The Ramones, and Cyndi Lauper.

After three years of meticulous renovations, the 16-room hotel opened in January 2025. The architecture, design, and craftsmanship were expertly executed by the Policronica agency. If you're drawn to Japanese minimalism and Nordic aesthetics, the Élysée Montmartre Hotel will feel like your sanctuary. The interior design embodies a philosophy of craftsmanship and bespoke detail, creating a space that is both serene and timeless.

Once a backstage haunt for rock legends, now a refined retreat shaped by design, detail, and soul.

AMOUR

Hôtel Amour

8 Rue de Navarin
75009 Paris

@hotelsamourparis
hotelamourparis.fr
+33 148 783180

The story of the Amour family began in May 2006 with the opening of Hôtel Amour in the Pigalle district, a stone's throw from Place St Georges and Place de Pigalle. At the time, three friends, Emmanuel Delavenne, Thierry Costes, and artist André Saraiva, discovered a private mansion in need of renovation, just a stone's throw from rue des Martyrs. They decided to transform it into a unique and welcoming space that reflected their own style. The result is now a Parisian classic: Hôtel Amour. The hotel's 28 rooms feature an eclectic collection of furniture, lovingly sourced over the years from antique dealers, auction houses, and flea markets. Many pieces were crafted by renowned decorators from the 1930s to 1950s. The walls are adorned with contemporary art and provocative, erotic imagery, giving the space its distinctive charm. Following the success of Hôtel Amour, the opening of a second, larger property was a natural next step. In November 2015, the trio launched Grand Amour in the 10th arrondissement, pouring their experience and creativity into this legendary space. In 2019, the Amour family opened their third hotel in the Fleurs district of Nice, just 200 metres from the iconic Negresco.

Hotel Amour is a love letter to the Paris you hope still exists.

GRAND
HOTEL
Amour

Hôtel Grand Amour

18 Rue de la Fidélité
75010 Paris

@hotelsamourparis
hotelamourparis.fr
+33 144 160330

After the success of Hôtel Amour, the three friends, Emmanuel Delavenne, Thierry Costes, and artist André Saraiva, decided in 2015 to open a second, larger property. For Grand Amour, located in the edgy 10th arrondissement, they combined their experience and creativity to create a truly legendary space. The name "Grand" Amour reflects its size, double that of Hôtel Amour. Maybe not the fanciest location, but these guys have the rare talent of finding the next hot spot. Plus, the fashionable Canal Saint-Martin is just a ten-minute walk from the hotel.

Each of the 42 accommodations, 41 rooms and a penthouse apartment at the top, has been decorated with contributions from artist friends, featuring vintage furniture, photographs, and artworks by icons such as Helmut Newton and Guy Bourdin. The all-day café/bistro is a vibrant hub, filled with artists, musicians, fashion industry professionals, families, travellers, and more.

Some places don't need to shout to be heard.
Hotel Grand Amour speaks in attitude, not volume.

Grand Pigalle Experimental

29 Rue Victor Massé
75009 Paris

@grandpigallehotel
grandpigalle.com
+33 185 731200

Grand Pigalle Experimental occupies a prime spot in Pigalle, inside a beautifully preserved Haussmann-style building. The hotel's 37 rooms reflect the renaissance of this historic district, featuring stylish, modern interiors by Dorothée Meilichzon. Each room captures the romantic spirit of Pigalle, with large bathtubs, warm gold accents, and private balconies overlooking the hotel's courtyard or the nearby rooftops of Paris and Montmartre.

The renowned restaurant Frenchie Pigalle on the ground floor is led by Michelin-starred chef Gregory Marchand, and one of three Frenchie restaurants in Paris. Step outside and you're in the heart of the Pigalle neighbourhood. Just around the corner, Rue des Martyrs offers an abundance of boulangeries, bistros, cheese and charcuterie shops, and a selection of cozy bars and cool vintage stores.

L'Eldorado

18 Rue des Dames
75017 Paris

@hoteleldoradoparis
hoteleldoradoparis.com
+33 145 223521

L'Eldorado is located in the charming Batignolles neighbourhood of the 17th arrondissement, offering a less touristy alternative to nearby Montmartre and Pigalle. It can best be described as a romantic boutique hotel with a relaxed country house ambiance, inspired by the nostalgic atmosphere of traditional family-run hotels found throughout France. The property underwent a dramatic transformation in 2023, led by Élodie and Pierre Moussié alongside Sophie Richard, the trio behind Hôtel Providence. The 26-room hotel, located at 18 Rue des Dames has retained its historic roots, but the design trio also added a modern aesthetic. All of the 26 rooms are uniquely designed, blending floral fabrics, Victorian details, 1950s-inspired furniture, and hand-crafted finishes by skilled artisans. The heart of the hotel is the courtyard, a tranquil retreat with palm trees, hydrangeas, ferns, and camellias. Shielded from the noise of city traffic, it's the perfect spot for dining or simply enjoying a drink from the cocktail menu.

L'Eldorado feels like a country house with a Parisian postcode.

Hôtel des Académies et des Arts

15 Rue de la Grande Chaumière
75006 Paris

@hoteldesacademiesetdesarts_
hoteldesacademies.fr
+33 143 266644

Tucked away in the heart of Paris' artistic district, between Saint-Germain-des-Prés and Montparnasse, lies the poetic Hôtel des Académies et des Arts. This 20-room boutique hotel, housed in an 18th-century building across from the Académie de la Grande Chaumière, once frequented by Buffet, Léger, and Foujita, aims to recreate the atelier atmosphere of Belle-Époque Paris. Carefully restored by architects Stéphanie Lizée and Raphaël Hugot, the hotel is a true homage to art. Everywhere you look, the works selected by the duo pay tribute to the illustrious artists who lived here or in the surrounding area, including Picasso, Modigliani, and Gauguin. Particularly impressive are the frescoes by Franck Lebraly, which adorn the ceilings of ten rooms, inspired by artists such as Pablo Picasso and Sonia Delaunay. But the engagement in art doesn't stop here. Hotel guests are even invited to join curated art workshops.

Nice to know: the beautiful art deco styled bathrooms have refillable toiletries from the French-owned brand Grown Alchemist.

Le Grand Hôtel Cayré

4 Bd Raspail
75007 Paris

@legrandhotelcayre
miirohotels.com/
legrandhotelcayre
+33 145 443888

Le Grand Hôtel Cayré, the flagship of lifestyle label Miiro, brings new life to a Saint-Germain icon. Recently restored by Michaelis Boyd, the hotel bridges 1920s elegance with a confident, contemporary take on Parisian style.

Its 123 rooms, including two suites, channel the feel of a well-loved Paris apartment: pale wood floors, vintage lighting, custom beds, and retro-tiled bathrooms complete with Le Labo products.

Le Grand Hôtel Cayré also pays homage to its storied past. Its brasserie, Annette, is named after French-German writer and pacifist Annette Kolb, who lived in the original Hôtel Cayré for 17 years. Enjoy classic French cuisine while soaking in views of Boulevard Raspail from the restaurant's terrace.

Hotel Piscine Molitor

13 Rue Nungesser et Coli
75016 Paris

@molitorparis
molitorparis.com
+ 33 156 070850

The stunning Art Deco building in Paris' 16th arrondissement comes with an impressive history. In 1929, Piscine Molitor opened its doors with an unforgettable inauguration featuring the two Olympic swimmers, Aileen Riggin Soule and Johnny "Tarzan" Weissmuller. With its two breathtaking swimming pools, the venue quickly became a magnet for Paris' young it-crowd and fashionable celebrities. Right up until the 1980s, Piscine Molitor was one of the city's hottest municipal pools, hosting everything from fashion shows and gala dinners to lavish pool parties.

In 1989, Molitor closed its doors, but it didn't stay quiet for long. Soon after, graffiti artists and ravers moved in, transforming the spectacular architectural space into a playground for street art and underground culture. In 2001, the rave collective Heretik held a massive party with over 5,000 attendees, solidifying Piscine Molitor's reputation as a hub for alternative art and music.

In 2014, after a huge refurbishment led by renowned French architect and designer Jean-Philippe Nuel, the building complex reopened as a modern boutique- and wellness hotel with 117 rooms and suites. While the venue now boasts modern upgrades like a 1,600 m² spa and an exclusive rooftop terrace, the building's iconic mustard-yellow façade remains untouched. The indoor and outdoor pools continues to be the heart of the hotel. Inside, the mix of contemporary design and Art Deco-inspired details serves as a striking reminder of the building's storied past and its cultural significance.

bar
hôtel

Le Pigalle

9 Rue Frochot
75009 Paris

@lepigalleparis
lepigalle.paris
+33 148 783714

Le Pigalle is a hotel born from the idea of creating a space that embodies the neighbourhood's tawdry charm, brazen spirit, and musical energy. Once a gritty Red-Light District, Pigalle was a chaotic blend of hookers, hustlers, and dreamers, a playground where artists, poets, and musicians soaked up the mesmerizing allure of nightlife to fuel their creativity.

Today, Pigalle has transformed into one of Paris' most sought-after neighbourhoods, and Le Pigalle perfectly captures the vibrant new atmosphere. The neoclassical building houses 40 individually designed rooms, inspired by the late 19th-century artists and poets who once roamed the area. Local artists and photographers contribute to the aesthetic; a classic low-key style, topped with cool 1950s and 1970s vintage furniture.

The hotel is still lit by the famous neon lights of the cabaret shows.

The Hoxton Paris

30-32 Rue du Sentier
75002 Paris

@thehoxtonhotel
thehoxton.com
+33 185 657500

Hoxton Hotels began, as the name suggests, in Hoxton, UK. Since then, the brand has brought its signature coolness to some of the trendiest cities across Europe and the US. Hoxton Paris became the fourth property in the Hoxton portfolio, opening its doors in the summer of 2017 in Paris' 2nd arrondissement.

The Hoxton brand owns this particular coolness that so many aspire to, but few truly achieve. Even though The Hoxton hotels maintain a consistent style and aesthetic, each property effortlessly integrates the history of its building and the distinctive character of the surrounding neighbourhood. This is especially true for Hoxton Paris.

Set in an 18th-century hôtel particulier, The Hoxton Paris occupies a magnificent building originally designed by architect Nicolas d'Orbay for Etienne Rivié. More recently, the property had served as a clothing factory before sitting vacant for a decade. After four years of meticulous renovation, The Hoxton brought this remarkable building back to life, blending its storied past with the brand's signature vibe.

The Hoxton doesn't chase cool, it sets the tone. This Paris outpost blends heritage with Hoxton's signature swagger. History never looked this sharp.

2

Union Boulangerie
Candle Kids Coffee
Sevenly Heart
Recto Verso
Dreamin' Man
Café Pigalle
Le Chateaubriand
Chez Georges
Amagat
Cafe Shin
Derriere
Early June
Septime
Clamato
Aux Deux Amis
Halo
Le Baratin
Deviant
Septime La Cave
Combat
Delicatessen Cave

Taste

Union Boulangerie

2 Rue Bleue
75009 Paris

@union_boulangerie

For Parisians, the bakery isn't just a place, it's part of daily life. From morning croissants to an afternoon goûter, a good boulangerie is a neighbourhood staple. That's exactly what Union Boulangerie set out to create when it opened in January 2021: a bakery rooted in tradition yet open to creativity, serving the local community with love and passion.

Inside, you'll find more than just beautifully baked bread. This is a place to gather, chat, and connect. The team at Union Boulangerie are more than bakers, they're keepers of culinary heritage, preserving time-honoured recipes while also experimenting with unexpected flavour pairings. Every loaf, every pastry, every delicate viennoiserie is crafted with care and precision. Ingredients are sourced locally and seasonally, supporting French farmers and showcasing the country's rich terroir.

Candle Kids Coffee

107 Rue des Couronnes
75020 Paris

@candlekidscoffee

At the top of Rue des Couronnes you'll find Candle Kids Coffee, a café with an unmistakable sense of home. Opened in 2023 by brothers Martin and Ernest (formerly at Marias concept store The Broken Arm) it blends Nordic minimalism with global inspiration, shaped by their travels from Seoul to São Paulo.

Inside, sunlight spills through bay windows onto cream-toned concrete and handcrafted wood, softened by beeswax candles and ceramic cups. The space was designed by Studio Ebur, who nailed that rare mix of serenity and character.

Ernest runs the kitchen, serving specialty coffee from Feve Roasters alongside house-made cinnamon rolls, canelés, and buttered toast. Don't miss the honeyed milk from the Chartreuse Valley or the cocoa infusion by Plaq, pure comfort in a cup.

Candle Kids feels more like a home than a café,
just with better pastries.

Sevenly Heart

55 Rue des Archives
75003 Paris

@sevenlyheart
sevenlyheart.com

Sevenly Heart is a charming café and wine bar in the heart of the Marais district in Paris. Since opening in 2023, it has quickly become a favourite among locals and a discerning creative crowd.

The space is celebrated for its highly aesthetic interior, where minimalist design meets vintage style. The centerpiece is the stone-carved desk, complemented by purposely unfinished walls, high ceilings, and carefully curated decor, and not least, their beautiful porcelain cups adorned with the signature red heart. It's no surprise that Sevenly Heart has sparked a serious buzz.

Surely, the café totally lives up to the hype. With its Instagram-worthy ambiance and delicious food, it's a spot that feels just as good as it looks.

During the day, Sevenly Heart serves specialty coffee and homemade pastries, including cookies, red velvet cake, and carrot cake. In the evening, the space transforms into a wine bar, offering a selection of wines paired with a nice selection of snacks.

LAPTOP?
NO THANKS
WE LOVE NOSTALGIA SO MUCH!

Recto Verso

6 Rue Portefoin
75003 Paris

@rectoversocafe

This cosy coffee spot in the heart of the Marais is a perennial favourite, no doubt about it. Opened in 2023 by creative partners Kevin Vasic and Luís Mesquita, the café is a reflection of their shared vision, intimate, intentional, and full of soul. Every detail, from the coffee to the interiors, is guided by a deep respect for craftsmanship and design.

Their approach to coffee is as thoughtful as everything else. Beans are sourced from top Nordic roasters, Norway's Fuglen and Sweden's Koppi, resulting in filter and espresso-based drinks that are precise, balanced, and quietly exceptional. The menu is complemented by a small selection of homemade pastries that have already earned cult status: the choco-macadamia cookie, a hojicha-infused cheesecake, and a shortbread topped with Plaq chocolate.

The branding is equally considered. A New York-based painter created the logo, while two cabinetmakers handcrafted the furniture and a Japanese ceramicist designed the tableware. The aesthetic is inspired by the minimal coffee bars of Tokyo and Seoul, but rooted in Parisian charm, elegant, understated, and full of warmth.

Tokyo vibes, Nordic beans, and pastries that might just ruin all others for you.

CIAO

ditting

Dreamin' Man

140 Rue Amelot
75011 Paris

@dreaminman_paris

Dreamin' Man coffee shop opened in Paris in 2019, founded by partners Yuichiro Sugiyama and Yui Matsuzaki, just a stone's throw from Place de la République in the 11th arrondissement. A tiny café packed with devastatingly cool people, it also carries a subtle Neil Young theme and a serious devotion to coffee. What a perfect mix!

The space is small, like really small. With just a handful of tables inside and a couple of sidewalk seats, arriving early is key. The interior is totally stylish, a mix of flea market finds, raw textures, and unfinished surfaces, creating a cozy, rustic vibe.

The real draw? That must be the coffee. Sugiyama swears by PROLOG, a Copenhagen-based roaster, using carefully sourced beans from Ethiopia, Kenya, and Colombia. His signature filtered coffee is brewed with precision and deep respect for the craft.

The pastry counter is equally thoughtful. Matsuzaki bakes daily, fig financiers, delicate Japanese pudding, and buttery cakes, all made with the freshest market finds.

In September 2022, Dreamin' Man expanded inside The Broken Arm in the Marais. The collaboration even inspired The Broken Arm to launch a "Dreamin' Man" T-shirt, further cementing their creative connection.

Café Pigalle

7 Rue Frochot
75009 Paris

@cafepigalleparis
lepigalle.paris/cafe-pigalle
+33 148 78 37 14

Located in Paris's Pigalle district, Café Pigalle is a relaxed and welcoming spot with a touch of character. Part of Le Pigalle Hotel, it's a favourite hangout for both locals and visitors looking for a good coffee or a laid-back meal. Whether it's an espresso, a latte, or a fresh pastry from a nearby bakery, the focus here is on simple, well-made food and drinks. Café Pigalle work with local suppliers and businesses to prepare food that offers something for everyone's palate, whether you're a Parisian or a passer-by, looking to dine in the restaurant or want to grab a snack on the street.

Open from morning until late, Café Pigalle shifts effortlessly from a daytime café to an easy-going evening spot. You can take a seat inside, grab a quick bite, or even slip into the hidden back room, perfect for a quiet dinner or small gathering. The menu reflects the neighbourhood's mix of influences, offering everything from a classic croque-monsieur to natural wines and cocktails.

Grab a coffee, cocktail, or a croque, it's all simple, good, and made with local love. Come for the vibe, stay for the secret back room.

Fanny Sabre · Maison Mosse · Jean Foillard · Marie Lassaigne · Famille Peyelat · Yoyo · Les Foulards Rouges · Iago
Domaine Anglore · Nicolas Renard · Christian Tschida · Maison Valette · S & A Cordeuil · Rapport Leroy · Beck Hartweg · JC Garnier
Gut Oggau · P&O Bonhomme · Claus Preisinger · Dario Princic · Valentin Morthanet · Radikon · Vouette & Sorbée · Vincent Laval · AMI
Benoit Courault · Thomas Santamaria · Ganevat · Richard Leroy · Les Bottes Rouges · Alex Foillard · C & JB Sénat · Fond Cyprès
Matthieu Barret · Adrien Berlioz · Dame Jeanne · John Okro · Alexandre Plassant · Julien Guillot · Brand Bros · Evelyne Clairet
Victoria Torres · Andreas Tscheppe · Famille Ligas · Calvez Bobinet · Léo Dirringer · Podere Pradarolo · Fred Gounan · Le Sorga
M & V Tricot · Patrick Bouju · Cruz Viejo · Alain Castex · Alexandre Bain · Nicolas Jacob · Strohmeier · A & O De Moor · Erich Andert
Seckinger · Imanol Garay · Vincent Ruiz · Didier Grappe · Domaine de Villeneuve · Philippe Viret · Laurent Bénard · Foradori · Selvadolce
Pierre Frick · Kumpf & Meyer · Milan Nestarec · Elvi Cedo · Brasserie des Voirons · Cantillon · des Frères Soulier · Famille Plageoles · Frantz Saumon
Les Capriades · Sylvain Sauve · Oscura · Olivier Boulin · Jacques Selosse · Famille Breton · Rémi Dufaitre · Tessa Laroche · Robin Carette
Margot & Natalia · Athénaïs de Béru · Catherine Riss · Hervé Souhaut · Famille Labet · Domaine Gramenon · JM Stephan · Cosmic
Jules Métras · Philippe Pacalet · Leila Pailhes · Es d'aqui · Esmeralda Garcia · Matassa · Yannick Meckert · Pheasant's Tears
Domaine Lissner · Octavin · Wilfried Garin · Mas Foulaquier · G Overnoy · Philippe Chatillon · Hervé Chaumet · David Fourrid · Arena

Le Chateaubriand

129 Ave Parmentier
75011 Paris

@lechateaubriand_
lechateaubriand.net
+33 143 574595

Established by chef Inaki Aizpitarte in 2006 in a then quite working-class neighborhood of Paris, the 11th arrondissement, Le Chateaubriand changed the history of gastronomy, offering a high-quality cuisine, with the same standards in terms of products and quality as a star-restaurant, madly creative and sometimes provocative, in a bistrot décor. The dining room remained almost untouched since the 1960s, and a very Parisian elegance comes from details such as the red benches, mirrors, lamps and golden curtains. The tasting menu, changing every week, includes five amuse-bouche, an entree, a fish course and a meat course, and two deserts. The wine list is amongst the best in Paris, featuring only natural wines, with a large choice of non-French wines. Le Chateaubriand also proposes a wine pairing allowing everyone to discover the cellar's best bottles. Nowadays chefs Daniel Savonarota and Leonardo Righini creates the menu at this true Parisian institution.

Chez Georges

1 Rue du Mail
75002 Paris

@chezgeorgesruedumail
+33 142 600711

A favourite bistro in Paris, not just mine, but everyone's who knows what's good. This place isn't just old-school, it owns it. Located into Rue du Mail, Chez Georges has been serving classic French bistro fare since the '60s and hasn't changed much since. Think steak-frites, leeks vinaigrette, and profiteroles the size of your head, all scribbled onto the paper tablecloth by brisk, black-vested waiters. It's loud, packed, and unapologetically French. The vibe is somewhere between power lunch and extended apéro, with a few regulars who look like they've been coming here since it opened and possibly have. It's the kind of spot that doesn't chase trends, because it is the reference. Come hungry, bring a sense of humour, and don't expect subtlety. Expect satisfaction, butter, and a very good story to tell after.

Amagat

23 Rue Villa Riberolle
75020 Paris

@amagat_paris
amagatparis.fr
+33 619 377131

At the bottom of Père-Lachaise Cemetery, where Belleville fades into Charonne, lies this treasure of a restaurant. Amagat is the kind of place you almost want to keep secret, a neighbourhood favourite disguised as a Catalan tavern. It's also one of my personal favourites.

Amagat combines French cuisine with Spanish tapas and Catalan wines. The chef has created a menu inspired by the flavors of his homeland. He blends classic dishes, such as bomba de Barceloneta and tortilla from his childhood, with more creative and inspired options, always staying true to the Catalan spirit. The choice of ingredients is also a central focus, with an emphasis on quality above all.

Come during the summer, when the courtyard is open, and you can sit outside all evening enjoying delicious cold wine and tasty tapas.

Café Shin

47 Rue des Petites Écuries
75010 Paris

@cafeshinparis
www.cafeshin.fr
+33 186 043368

You might think that Paris has a café on every corner, but compared to Seoul, it's really nothing. With nearly 20,000 cafés, the South Korean capital holds the title for the highest number of cafés per capita in the world. So, it makes perfect sense to open a fully Korean-style café in Paris.

Drawing on their years of collaboration at Créatures, Forest, and more recently in the kitchens of Micho, Julien Sebbag and his pastry chef friend Shin Eun Jung have sealed their partnership by joining forces to open the brand-new Café Shin. This space challenges the established codes of Parisian savoir-vivre, drawing inspiration the modern and original café concepts of Shin's home country, South Korea.

Café Shin is located in the heart of the 10th arrondissement, bringing life to this more laid-back neighbourhood. At the counter, you'll find a variety of traditional and specialty coffees, served hot or iced, alongside indulgent pastries and kimbap as a savoury lunch option, taking guests on a journey to the East in no time.

The duo collaborated with Seoul-based Alphabet Agency for the visuals, while Uchronia Studio oversaw the interior architecture. Together, they've created a next-generation coffee shop that feels like a perfect blend of Paris and Seoul.

This place rewrites the Paris coffee script with a bold Korean twist. It's East meets West, and it actually works harmoniously.

Club Med
RISE
forlife

Derrière

69 Rue des Gravilliers
75003 Paris

@restaurantderriere
derriere-resto.com
+33 144 619195

Hidden behind a storefront and accessed via an alley that opens into a small courtyard, Derrière is a true speakeasy-style spot tucked deep in the Marais district. The restaurant is run by brothers Mourad and Hakim Mazouz, the masterminds behind this extraordinary dining experience.

Inside, you can choose between various rooms: sit in the living room with a live ping-pong table, lounge on a mattress in the bedroom, or retreat to the boudoir—or one of several other quirky chambers. A smoking lounge is hidden behind a secret doorway for those who fancy an after-dinner cigarette.

Chef Lionel Delage brings authentic French culinary finesse to a modern menu. Comfort food reigns supreme, with steak frites a proud dinner staple and a lavish weekend brunch to match. Derrière is an Instagram favourite, outrageously trendy, yet genuinely impressive, with excellent food and an exceptional overall experience.

It’s wild, weird, and unexpectedly delicious. Like a dinner party thrown by someone with too many rooms and excellent taste.

Explorations in College Algebra

Early June

19 Rue Jean Poulmarch
75010 Paris

@earlyjuneparis
earlyjune.fr
+33 142 854074

A small and incredibly cozy restaurant and wine bar nestled in the charming Canal Saint-Martin district. What makes Early June unique is its chef-in-residence concept, where a new guest chef takes over the kitchen each month. Probably a nightmare for any food critic, but it creates a rare, dynamic atmosphere where every visit is unique.

The ambiance feels like being in a warm, welcoming living room among good friends. The interior embraces the neo-bistro aesthetic, with vintage furniture, raw textures, and unpolished surfaces.

You can choose to sit inside with a view of the open kitchen or grab one of the few outdoor seats overlooking the canal. Just make sure to arrive early, reservations are only accepted for groups of four or more.

Because of its constantly changing kitchen, Early June has no set menu. Instead, guests are treated to seasonal small plates that reflect the vision of the current chef. Expect everything from vegetable-forward dishes to seafood and meat, always paired with a carefully curated natural wine, though you can safely leave the decision-making to the sommelier.

No set menu, just seasonal plates, good wine, and the feeling you've walked into someone's very chic living room.

19
EARLY
JUNE

Septime

80 Rue de Charonne
75011 Paris

@septimeparis
Septime-charonne.fr

The first and most renowned restaurant by star chef Bertrand Grébaut, Septime offers a one-star Michelin fine dining experience that is far removed from the often pretentious style you might typically encounter.

Like its sister restaurant, Clamato, Septime embraces an understated, rustic Nordic style, free of tablecloths and unnecessary frills. The interior features reclaimed wood tables, industrial lighting, exposed concrete, and glass, epitomizing the modern industrial trend.

Septime is a pioneer of the neo-bistro movement, breathing new life into traditional French gastronomy by blending it with contemporary techniques, trends, and bold flavors.

Lunch consists of a five-course tasting menu, while dinner offers a seven-course experience—both paired with an exceptional wine menu.

A word to the wise: reservations go fast. Don't make the rookie mistake of thinking this is just another chic spot. Septime is the kind of place food lovers fly in for.

Rustic, refined, and quietly revolutionary,
this is fine dining stripped of ego and full of soul.

Clamato

80 Rue de Charonne
75011 Paris

@septimeparis
clamato-charonne.fr
+33 143 727453

To be honest, I don't agree when people say they went to Clamato because there was no table available at Septime. Clamato is an outstanding restaurant that is easily on par with Septime, offering a menu by Bertrand Grébaut focused on fish and shellfish. The logo reveals Grébaut's flair for graphic design, a field he studied before starting his career in the restaurant business. The style also shows clear inspiration from classic oyster bars on the American East Coast—and I've been to a few of them, this one holds water.

You just have to love this place for its honest simplicity. The ingredients are carefully selected and prepared as simply as possible, served on sharing plates.

Much like the menu, the interior is totally understated but in a super trendy way. Vintage chairs, benches, and worn wooden tables are paired with plastered walls complemented by a beautiful dark green hue. Please note that reservations are not possible, so make sure to arrive early.

No reservations, no pretence, just
very good food done very, very right.

Neighbourhoods

Bastille / Oberkampf / Charonne
Canal Saint-Martin
Belleville
Pigalle / Opera
Louvre
Marais
Bourse
Saint-Germain-des-Prés

Paris

A cityscape is defined by the sum of its neighbourhoods. They are the heartbeat of a city, infusing life and diversity into its very soul. Some are artsy and vibrant, others are more serene and exclusive. Each neighbourhood has its own unique character, and we all have our favourite areas that we feel connected to. In this section, we break down the city and introduce you to the coolest neighbourhoods. All the locations in the book, along with a few bonus spots, are marked on detailed neighbourhood maps, making it easy for you to discover your favourite district.

5
10
6
8
4
9
7
2
3
1
11

Bastille / Oberkampf / Charonne

			Don't Miss:
1	Galerie Patrick Seguin (p. 117)	9	Bambino, 25 Rue Saint-Sébastien, 75011 Paris
2	Clamato (p. 95)	10	Folderol, 10 Rue du Grand Prieuré, 75011 Paris
3	Septime (p. 91)	11	Bistro Paul Bert, 18 Rue Paul Bert, 75011 Paris
4	Aux Deux Amis (p. 99)		
5	Le Chateaubriand (p. 71)		
6	Dreamin' Man (p. 65)		
7	Septime La Cave (p. 111)		
8	Delicatessen Cave (p. 119)		

The lively 11th arrondissement can be divided into three main areas: Bastille, Oberkampf, and Charonne. Located east of the Seine, it stretches between Place de la Bastille, Père Lachaise, Belleville, and Place de la Nation. This neighbourhood is beloved by Parisians for its vibrant nightlife, concert venues, and exceptional dining options.

Your journey through the 11th begins at Place de la Bastille, where the Colonne de Juillet monument stands at its centre. This historic square once housed the infamous Bastille prison, playing a pivotal role during the French Revolution in the 18th century. Just north of Bastille is Oberkampf, a hotspot for bars and live music venues, with the Bataclan being the most iconic. Though sadly associated with the 2015 terror attack, the venue remains a must-visit for some of the best live shows in Paris. Don't let its history deter you from experiencing this legendary concert hall. Charonne with its trendy restaurants and bars, is one of the city's best areas for a night out. Highlights include Clamato and Septime, as well as their renowned wine bar, Septime La Cave, regarded as one of the top natural wine spots in Paris.

Further along Rue de Charonne you reach Père Lachaise, where cultural icons like Jim Morrison and Edith Piaf, who once lived in the 11th, are buried.

1
6
5
8
7
2
10
9
3
4

Canal Saint Martin

				Don't miss:
1	Hotel Grand Amour (p. 25)		8	Le Citizen Hotel, 96 Quai de Jemmapes, 75010 Paris
2	Centre Commercial (p. 127)		9	La Trésorerie, 11 Rue du Château d'Eau, 75010 Paris
3	Thanx God I'm a V.I.P. (p. 145)		10	Boulangerie Du Pain et Des Idées, 34 Rue Yves Toudic, 75010 Paris
4	The Next Door (p. 153)			
5	Déviant (p. 107)			
6	Cafe Shin (p. 79)			
7	Early June (p. 87)			

Canal Saint-Martin stretches across the 10th and 11th arrondissements, connecting the Canal de l'Ourcq with the Seine. Constructed in the early 1800s, the canal was originally designed to bring fresh drinking water and transport goods into Paris. Today, the area around Canal Saint-Martin is the coolest neighbourhood, bustling with shops, restaurants, cafés and wine bars. Especially during the summer, the Canal district comes alive with people lounging along its banks, soaking up the sun, and enjoying apéros and picnics. The lively atmosphere is driven primarily by local residents rather than tourists, allowing the neighbourhood to maintain its authentic, local charm.

Canal Saint-Martin is also home to some of Paris's best concept stores, including The Next Door and Centre Commercial. For vintage fashion enthusiasts, Thanx God I'm a V.I.P. is an absolute must-visit.

VHF
20

4
1
3
6
7
5
2

Belleville

Don't miss:

1 Le Baratin (p. 105)
2 Amagat (p. 75)
3 Candle Kids Coffee (p. 55)
4 Combat (p. 115)
5 Mama Shelter Paris East, 109 Rue de Bagnolet, 75020 Paris
6 Rue Denoyez, Rue Denoyez, 75020 Paris
7 Parc de Belleville, 47 Rue des Couronnes, 75020 Paris

Once a gritty, working-class area in northeastern Paris, Belleville was long overlooked by tourists, except for those who stumbled upon it after visiting the famed Père-Lachaise Cemetery. Today, it's shaking off its somehow seedy reputation and emerging as one of the city's most exciting neighbourhoods. Previously overshadowed by the trendier 10th and 11th arrondissements, Belleville is now luring a young, creative crowd away from the bourgeois vibes of the natural wine-heavy 11th. With more affordable rents and a raw, unpolished charm, it's carving out a unique identity.

Belleville is a true melting pot, home to Armenian and Tunisian Jews, Greeks, Chinese, and Southeast Asian communities. This cultural diversity creates a vibrant atmosphere, with quirky mom-and-pop shops and family-run restaurants along Rue de Belleville. Head up the hill for stunning Eiffel Tower views.

It's also a foodie haven, boasting everything from neo-bistros and multicultural gems like Lao Siam to classic French fare at Le Baratin, Belleville's first natural wine bistro.

4
5
1
6
3
2
8
9
7

Pigalle / Opera

			Don't Miss:
1	Le Pigalle (p. 43)	8	Rose Bakery, 46 R. des Martyrs, 75009 Paris
2	Hotel Amour (p. 21)	9	Le Pain Retrouvé, 18 R. des Martyrs, 75009 Paris
3	Grand Pigalle Experimental (p. 29)	10	Frenchie Pigalle, 29 Rue Victor Massé, 75009 Paris
4	L'Eldorado (p. 31) 17 arr		
5	Élysée Montmartre (p. 17) 18 arr		
6	Café Pigalle (p. 67)		
7	Union Boulangerie (p. 53)		

Pigalle sits at the foot of Montmartre, just a stone's throw from the tourist-laden Sacré-Coeur Basilica. Once a gritty red-light district infamous for its sex shops, cabarets, and the iconic Moulin Rouge, Pigalle has undergone a dramatic transformation. Today, it's one of the trendiest districts in Paris, rivalling the Marais in both style and scene.

The area affectionately dubbed SoPi (South Pigalle) is the epicentre of the trendy Pigalle. Framed by the Blanche and Anvers metro stations on one end and Notre-Dame-de-Lorette and Trinité-d'Estienne-d'Orves on the other, this grid encapsules the creative energy of the area. At the centre lies Rue des Martyrs, surrounded by cool bakeries, third-wave coffee bars, fashion-forward boutiques and neo-bistros.

Next to Pigalle is the Opéra district, and just beyond that, the two legendary department stores: Galeries Lafayette and Printemps.

LIGNES
Nos 2·12

LIGNES
Nos 2·12

1
2
3
4
5
7
8

Louvre

1 Bourse de Commerce — The Pinault Collection (p. 167)
2 Musée des Arts Décoratifs (p. 189)
3 Musée de l'Orangerie (p. 179)
4 Merci #2, 19 Rue de Richelieu, 75001 Paris

Don't miss:

5 Bode Paris, 6 Rue de Valois, 75001 Paris
6 Le Centre Pompidou, Place Georges-Pompidou, 75004 Paris
7 Louvre, 75001 Paris
8 Comptoir de la Gastronomie, 34 Rue Montmartre, 75001 Paris

From Place de la Concorde to the Centre Pompidou, the 1st arrondissement stretches along the Seine, with the Louvre Museum and the Tuileries Gardens serving as majestic focal points that showcase Paris's royal splendour from the era before the country became a republic.

The 1st arrondissement is brimming with culture, art, and history. The world's largest museum, the Louvre, is naturally a must-see, if you don't mind the long queues. Alternatively, you can visit the Musée des Arts Décoratifs, dedicated to design and decorative arts, or admire Monet's peaceful water lily series at the Musée de l'Orangerie. The two streets, Rue de Rivoli and Rue Saint-Honoré, form the neighbourhood's main commercial arteries. Rue Saint-Honoré, in particular, was once Paris's central fashion street, and although it can no longer claim that title, it's still a fantastic street to stroll through.

1
2
3
4
5
6
7
8
9
10
11

Marais

1 Merci (p. 137)
2 Yvon Lambert Gallery (p. 151)
3 The Broken Arm (p. 147)
4 Dover Street Market (p. 129)
5 Jimmy Fairly (p. 131)
6 Words Sounds Colors & Shapes (p. 157)
7 Recto Verso (p. 61)
8 Musée National Picasso-Paris (p. 185)
9 Lafayette Antipication (p. 181)
10 Derriére (p. 83)
11 Sevenly Heart (p. 59)

Marais stretches across the 3rd and 4th arrondissements, from the Centre Pompidou to Place des Vosges. Originally, Marais was inhabited by the French aristocracy, but later, at the end of the 19th century, the Jewish community arrived, turning Marais into a commercial district. During the 1980s, Marais was discovered by the LGBTQ+ community in Paris, and the neighbourhood developed into the city's most influential creative quarter. From here, the trendy café culture emerged, which was later exported to all other major cities. Even today, Marais is still the epitome of fashionable Paris with its many cafés, restaurants, and trendy shops.

1
2
3
4
5
6

Bourse

			Don't Miss:
1	The Hoxton Paris (p. 47)	4	Hotel Hana, 17 Rue du 4 septembre, 75002 Paris
2	Halo (p. 101)	5	Harry's New York Bar, 5 Rue Daunou, 75002 Paris
3	Chez Georges (p. 73)	6	Galerie Vivienne, 4 Rue des Petits Champs, 75002 Paris

The 2nd arrondissement, known as Bourse, which means "stock exchange" in French, is the financial heart of the city. However, it's also the smallest arrondissement, offering charm and character beyond its business credentials. Its key attractions include the Bourse de Commerce, the former stock exchange, transformed into a museum in 2021, and the stunning covered passage of Galerie Vivienne. Less touristy than the 1st arrondissement, the 2nd has a uniquely village-like atmosphere, with its pedestrian-only streets and covered passages.

9
12
8
5
3
7
6
4
11
2
10
1

Saint-Germain-Des-Prés

			Don't Miss:
1	Hotel Piscine Molitor (p. 41)	11	Smallable, 81 Rue du Cherche-Midi, 75006 Paris
2	Hôtel des Académies et des Arts (p. 35)	12	Petibon, 24 Rue du 4 Septembre, 75002 Paris
3	Le Grand Hotel Cayré (p. 39)		
4	Le Bon Marché (p. 135)		
5	Arrogant Verneuil (p. 123)		
6	Saint Laurent Babylone (p. 141)		
7	Amelie du Chalard Gallery (p. 163)		
8	Palais de Tokyo (p. 191)		
9	Fondation Louis Vuitton (p. 173)		
10	Fondation Cartier (p. 171)		

Located on the Left Bank, Saint-Germain-des-Prés is part of the 7th arrondissement, stretching west towards the Eiffel Tower. In the 1960s, Saint-Germain-des-Prés was the meeting place for intellectuals, writers, artists and musicians. They gathered here to work, converse, and find inspiration. Icons such as Jean-Paul Sartre, Simone de Beauvoir, Boris Vian, Guillaume Apollinaire, Albert Camus, and even Pablo Picasso made this area their creative hub.

Today, the Left Bank is more luxurious. The progressive crowd has long since migrated to northern Paris, and Saint-Germain-des-Prés has transformed into the epitome of chic, brimming with upscale boutiques, elegant cafés, and fine dining restaurants. The main street, Boulevard Saint-Germain, is now renowned for its fashion boutiques and showrooms featuring major designer brands.

Don't miss Paris' most exclusive department store, Le Bon Marché, along with the many other exceptional spots highlighted in this guide, more than enough to spend an inspiring day exploring the Left Bank.

LE CRIN
PEGGY MELLA
UNDER CUT

Aux Deux Amis

45 Rue Oberkampf
75011 Paris

@auxdeuxamis
+33 158 303813

Aux Deux Amis represents everything that's good in life: a certain idea of pleasure, carefree enjoyment, and warm humanity. Deranged minds might indeed see this terrace, occupied by some of the most beautiful people in Paris, and fully bearded hipster men, as a true threat to old-fashioned civilization. Or they might consider that this narrow spot, bordered by a bar with formica counters heavily stocked with natural wines, Iberian ham, and tortillas, is the most depraved representation of a world of miscreants. Yet it's a world that stands tall, regathering its strength whenever needed, in both good times and bad.

David Loyola, the owner, has built a place where guests feel good, where a certain roughness in the welcome and the way the dishes are served is softened with smiles, playful banter, and loyalty. This is one of the quintessentially Parisian spots that doesn't reveal itself easily. It must be approached, appreciated, and revisited to truly grasp its intensity and to sense the careful alchemy that combines a cuisine never lacking in character, sometimes, yes, a bit cheeky, but rarely so, and one of the best wine cellars in Paris.

Halo

12 Rue Saint-Sauveur
75002 Paris

@haloparis.co
halo-paris.com

The 2nd arrondissement, also known as The Bourse district, is nestled between the elegant 1st arrondissement and the edgier 10th arrondissement. But Bourse is not to be underestimated, it has its own standout spots, and Halo is undoubtedly one of them.

Housed in the historic Hôtel d'Osmont, this unique space blends gastronomy, design, and history under one spectacular pyramidal glass roof, an architectural nod to the Eiffel era.

The restaurant shares its space with a cutting-edge concept store, where emerging designers influence everything from the ceramic tableware to the staff uniforms, all available for purchase. The minimalist yet rich interior, designed by Lucie Rosenblatt of mur.mur architects, enhances the building's 18th-century charm without overshadowing its past.

The chef, Victor Blanchet, has a résumé that includes Alain Passard's L'Arpège, Neso, and Top Chef 2023. In other words, he is really good! His cuisine is a delicious blend of Mediterranean and Basque influences.

Part restaurant, part concept store. Expect bold cooking, curated ceramics, and a space that feels as thoughtful as the food.

LE BARATIN

Le Baratin

3 Rue Jouye-Rouve
75020 Paris

@lebaratinparis
+33 143 493970

Food and wine pilgrims, particularly those who read the New York Times or watch Anthony Bourdain, are willing to climb the hill for this Belleville institution.

Argentine chef Raquel Carena pretty much invented "bistronomy," as many young chefs acknowledge. This stripped-down, retro bistro serves food that is delicate or hearty, but always personal. The blackboard menu makes pleasant reading, the prices are restrained and the wines appealing. Reservations strongly recommended.

Le Baratin (which oddly means 'sales pitch' or 'sweet talk') is hidden in amongst the labyrinth of Belleville and used to be a well-kept secret among chefs and foodies alone, a haven where (as rumour has it) local chefs dine in their off time. Since being published in Le Guide Michelin, amongst others, the restaurant has become a trendy destination for travellers and, as it were, annoying food bloggers, however chef Raquel Carena and her partner and resident wine connoisseur Philipp Pinoteu, have not let popularity get in the way of quality. This is a Paris institution for a reason.

Déviant

39 Rue des Petites Écuries
75010 Paris

@deviantgram
deviant.paris
+33 140 00 21 24

Déviant is Vivant 2's naughty little brother, a cave out back with no bookings, only standing space, and an ironic misfit's approach to small plates and natural wine.

Maybe you've heard of Vivant, a hotspot among cool Parisians from day one. Well, the talented chef Pierre Touitou has done it again with Déviant, one of the trendiest bars in Paris, on Rue des Petites Écuries in the 10th arrondissement.

Every evening, the show begins as the iron curtain rises, unveiling a striking black-and-white marble bar, completely open to the street. The simple stage is set: no walls, no doors, no tables. Just a lively crowd spilling onto the pavement, sipping natural wine, laughing, and sharing small plates on sleek countertops. Obviously, the wines are all organic.

No tables, no bookings, no problem. It's chaos, it's charm, and it works beautifully.

MAGNUMS
BRUTAL TSCHIDA
TERRE D'OMBRE. L'ANGLORE
MARANGES. SEXTANT
CHASSIGNOL. THILLARDON
ET PLEIN D'AUTRES...

Septime La Cave

3 Rue Basfroi
75011 Paris

@septimeparis
septime-lacave.fr
+33 143 671487

The famous triangle on Rue de Charonne consists of Septime, Clamato, and Septime la Cave. Septime ranks among the best restaurants in Paris, probably the best in town. Clamato matches its more famous big brother in quality, while the wine bar Septime la Cave is the trendy younger sister. It's the perfect spot to start the evening with a glass of wine, wrap it up, or simply stay all night, thanks to their small but delicious charcuterie and cheese menu.

The clientele is young and stylish, and the place is often packed, but when that happens, the party just spills out onto the street. The wine selection leans heavily toward small producers, with a focus on biodynamic and natural wines. They always have 10 different wines by the glass, which change regularly. The bartenders know their stuff and are more than happy to help you find the perfect wine.

Ten glasses on rotation, snacks that hit the spot,
and a crowd that's just as polished as the pours.

29
13
BEAUJOLAIS VILLAGES
NOUVEAU
2011
Festivitas

Combat

63 Rue de Belleville
75019 Paris

@combat_bellebille
+33 980 847860

The kind of place where you go for just one drink... and somehow stay for nine more.

Combat is a cool yet completely unpretentious cocktail bar in the heart of Belleville, right across from Place Fréhel. Since opening in summer 2017, it has quickly gained a reputation as the best bar in Belleville.

Owned and run by Elena Schmitt and Margot Lecarpentier, the bar was founded with a clear mission: to challenge the male-dominated bar scene, bring feminine values and aesthetics into the mix, and, above all, create a safe, cozy, and inclusive space.

The minimalist interior keeps things simple: white walls, mustard-yellow tiles behind the stainless-steel bar, and lush greenery hanging from the ceiling, all lightly scented with eucalyptus. Thanks to floor-to-ceiling windows, you instantly get a feel for the relaxed, effortlessly cool crowd inside.

Cocktails at Combat are top-notch, focusing on quality over quantity. The menu is concise, but every drink is a winner. A selection of snackable bites, cheese, olives, feta, and artichokes, rounds out the experience.

No frills, no fuss, just bold flavours
and good energy.

GIN
Préface
Préface

Delicatessen Cave

136 Rue de Amalot
75011 Paris

@delicatessencave
septime-lacave.fr
+33 981 643367

What started as a small wine shop in 2016 has grown into a Parisian institution. Mireille Langlois opened Delicatessen Cave in July 2016 with just 50 carefully chosen wines. A year later, her son Gabriel joined her, and together they built a cellar that now boasts over 1,200 references, sourced exclusively from winemakers they know personally, producers who respect the land and all living things.

For the past eight years, they've been open seven days a week, attracting a clientele that ranges from local neighbors to wine lovers from around the world. In 2022, they expanded across the street with Delicatessen Place, a laid-back wine bar open daily from 5 PM to 10 PM, featuring talented chefs and an outstanding front-of-house team.

Inside the former shoe repair shop, the green façade and vintage "Cordonnerie Derby" sign welcome guests into a space filled with exposed concrete, wooden walls, and hanging Edison bulbs. Here, guests sip on natural wine and enjoy buffet-style small plates, from hand-selected cheeses and charcuterie to the shop's stellar bubbly selection.

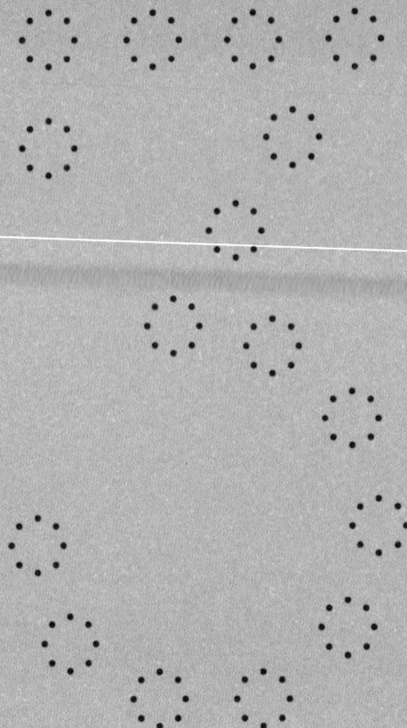

Arrogant Verneuil

Centre Commercial

Dover Street Market

Jimmy Fairly

Le Bon Marche

Merci

Saint Laurent Babylone

Thanx God I'm a V.I.P

The Broken Arm

Yvon Lambert Gallery

The Next Door

Words Sounds Colors & Shapes

Shop

Arrogant Verneuil

60 Rue de Verneuil
75007 Paris

@arrogantverneuil
arrogant-paris.com
+31 653 96 93 25

One of my friends introduced me to this very special place a few years ago. Calling Arrogant Verneuil a shop would be an understatement. Perhaps the best way to describe it, without exaggeration, is as a magical experience. Stepping inside feels like entering a scene from One Thousand and One Nights, where art, design, and storytelling merge into an enchanting universe.

The story behind Arrogant Verneuil begins with Rozemarijn de Witte, former Linda editor, who, after selling her publishing company, embarked on a creative journey with her husband, former basketball player Pierre Traversier. They first transformed an abandoned hotel in Ibiza into Los Enamorados and later set their sights on Paris, reinventing a Left Bank space into Arrogant Verneuil, a boutique, gallery, and home in one.

Located in Paris' 7th arrondissement, the store is a curated cabinet of curiosities, filled with vintage furniture, ceramics, art, and fashion. The gallery, also their private residence, is open by appointment only, featuring a carefully curated art collection in a space blending industrial charm and refined craftsmanship.

Make sure to spend some time in the 7th arrondissement, one of my favourites, thanks to its antique shops, nice galleries, and that special Left Bank charm.

ALENTEJO

Centre Commercial

2 Rue de Marseille
75010 Paris

@centre_commercial
centrecommercial.cc
+33 142 022608

Centre Commercial should always be at the top of your shopping list in Paris. It's one of my must-visit stops whenever I'm in Canal Saint-Martin.

Centre Commercial opened its doors in 2010 in the Canal Saint-Martin district, founded by Sébastien Kopp and François-Ghislain Morillion, the duo behind the ethical sneaker brand VEJA. More than a boutique, it's a curated lifestyle space blending consciously made fashion with vintage furniture, art books, vinyl, and indie zines. A concept store with a conscience.

Their fashion collection is a carefully curated selection of brands from France, Denmark, and Great Britain, all with a strong focus on local production, an essential part of their philosophy. Additionally, it serves as a collective space, bringing together local, social, and environmental initiatives.

In 2013, Centre Commercial Kids was launched, offering sustainable fashion for children and reinforcing the brand's commitment to conscious consumption across generations. In summer 2025, Centre Commercial will expand its universe with an outdoor store just down the street on 10 Rue de Marseille.

Dover Street Market

37 Rue des Francs Bourgeois
75004 Paris

@doverstreetmarketparis
doverstreetmarketparis.com
+33 184 750500

Dover Street Market opened its first store in London in 2004, expanding globally under the leadership of Adrian Joffe and Rei Kawakubo. Despite opening in Tokyo, New York, Singapore, Beijing, and Los Angeles, Paris, fashion's epicentre, was repeatedly overlooked.

After testing the waters with DSM Little Market and DSM Perfume Market, the decision was made. In May 2024, Dover Street Market finally arrived in Paris, opening in the historic 17th-century Hôtel de Coulanges in the Hotel de Ville / Marais district.

Designed entirely by Rei Kawakubo, the space is stark and minimalist, no decorations, no logos, and no garments visible from the street. Instead, the 1,100 m², three-floor boutique is an immersive experience where design takes precedence.

As with other DSM locations, Rose Bakery offers a cosy spot to relax. The curated brand selection includes Comme des Garçons, alongside exclusives for France like Willy Chavarria, Rick Owens, Niccolò Pasqualetti, Simone Rocha, Bottega Veneta, and Wales Bonner.

JIMMY FAIRLY

Jimmy Fairly

3 Rue de Bretagne
75003 Paris

@jimmyfairly
jimmyfairly.com

Jimmy Fairly is a well-known eyewear brand in France, but despite its many stores, it is still relatively young. It was founded in 2010 in Toulouse by two young entrepreneurs, Sacha Bostoni and Antonin Chartier.

From the beginning, their bold mission was to offer high-quality prescription glasses at an affordable price, challenging an optical industry controlled by a handful of multinational companies maintaining artificially high prices.

The brand is driven by the belief that everyone has the right to clear vision. For each pair of glasses purchased, another is donated to a person in need through organisations such as Emmaüs.

To celebrate their 100th location, they took things up a notch with a space designed to highlight their sustainable commitments while looking toward the future. In the heart of the Upper Marais, next to the Marché des Enfants Rouges and surrounded by galleries and pop-up stores, the Jimmy Fairly boutique on Rue de Bretagne is a pink-hued space inspired by the iconic sci-fi movie *2001: A Space Odyssey*.

The name "Jimmy Fairly" was inspired by a Ben & Jerry's ice cream flavour called "Fairly Nuts" and was paired with the iconic actor James Dean, whose nickname was Jimmy.

la prairie

Le Bon Marche

24 Rue de Sèvres
75007 Paris

@lebonmarcherivegauche
lebonmarche.com
+33 144 398000

The first department store in history, Le Bon Marché Rive Gauche, was founded in 1852 by Marguerite and Aristide Boucicaut, a visionary couple who laid the groundwork for modern commerce. Today, the store spans two buildings and nearly 40,000 square metres, offering an extensive selection of products across women's, men's, and children's fashion, accessories, tableware, and design, along with a dedicated space for urban mobility.

For over 170 years, arts and entertainment have been woven into the DNA of Le Bon Marché Rive Gauche, brought to life through cultural exhibitions, concerts, and artist encounters held throughout the year within the store. Gastronomy also holds a special place here, with La Grande Épicerie de Paris celebrating its 100th anniversary in 2023.

Merci
MERCI

Merci

111 Bd Beaumarchais
75003 Paris

19 Rue de Richelieu
75001 Paris

@merciparis
merci-merci.com
+33 142 770033

Excellence in curation, that's the essence of Merci, Paris's most influential concept store. The rightful successor to the now-closed Colette. Tucked away off Boulevard Beaumarchais in the high Marais district, first-time visitors might be surprised to find that you enter the store by passing through a narrow gate and into a courtyard. There, you'll be greeted by the store's mascot, a tiny red Fiat 500 with a number plate that reads "Merci". Inside, Merci unveils itself across three floors, showcasing a true masterclass in what modern retail spaces are all about: inspiration, curation, and experience.

It's a true display of the art of curation, where visitors are continually fascinated by the store's unique selection of products sourced from near and far. From fashion, interior design, furniture, cosmetics, and books to textiles, Merci has developed its own style and identity that customers from all over the world connect to. In recent years, Merci own lifestyle merchandise collection has expanded significantly. Once limited to tote bags and caps, the iconic red Merci logo now covers a much larger product portfolio.

In March 2025 Merci opened a new second store at 19 Rue de Richelieu in the 1st arrondissement.

Merci has rewritten the rulebook on concept stores, and framed it beautifully.

Merci's
Cartoon
Palace

VIVIANE
LE CORBUSIER
PIERRE JEANNERET
LIGHTOPIA
JEAN-MICHEL

Saint Laurent Babylone

9 Rue de Grenelle
75007 Paris

@saintlaurentbabylone
ysl.com
+33 145 44 39 01

Saint Laurent Babylone is a new cultural destination and bookstore in the heart of Paris, dedicated to art, culture, and new modes of expression.

Created by Saint Laurent Creative Director Anthony Vaccarello, this new incarnation of Saint Laurent Rive Droite offers a diverse and globe-spanning collection of books, art, and music, as well as a new genre of cultural space.

Saint Laurent Babylone is a gathering place for artistic innovators, where connections and ideas can be born. More than a traditional bookstore, the space offers an unparalleled collection of books, art, and music and serves as a destination for cultural events, including DJ sessions, author readings, and signings.

Saint Laurent Babylone is named in homage to the Sèvres-Babylone neighborhood, where Yves Saint Laurent and Pierre Bergé once resided.

HARMONY

Thanx God I'm a V.I.P.

12 Rue de Lancry
75010 Paris

@thanxgodimavip
thanxgod.com
+33 142 030209

The first thing that catches the eye is the name, Thanx God I'm a VIP. A playful nod to owner Sylvie Chateigner's past life as a doorwoman in '90s Paris, where she was endlessly bombarded with people insisting on their VIP status. In 1994 she opened her first boutique with high fashion and sometimes wild parties, quickly drawing in the city's creative crowd. The shop eventually closed in 1998, but her love for vintage never faded.

A decade later Thanx God I'm a VIP made its grand return. This time, Chateigner, alongside her partner Amnaye Nhas, set up shop in the 10th arrondissement, tucked away on a quiet side street near République.

Inside is every vintage lover's dream. Everything is sorted by colour, turning the space into a visual feast of deep emerald greens, royal blues, buttery caramels, and classic Parisian blacks. The racks are filled with gems from Prada, Chanel, Hermès, Burberry, Thierry Mugler, and Lacroix, curated with an eye for pieces that feel just as relevant today as when they first hit the runway.

And it doesn't stop at one shop. Thanx God I'm a VIP has expanded into three boutiques on Rue de Lancry, one dedicated to womenswear, another for menswear, and a third for homewares and children's pieces.

BROKEN

The Broken Arm

12 Rue Perrée
75003 Paris

@thebrokenarm
the-broken-arm.com
+33 144 615360

The Broken Arm is a multi-label boutique located on Rue Perrée, right in the heart of the Marais district in Paris. Its story began with a prophetically named website, Des Jeunes Gens Modernes (Modern Young Things), which challenged and commented on all aspects of modernity, from fashion to food.

In 2013, three members of the collective, Anaïs Lafarge, Romain Joste, and Guillaume Steinmetz, took things a step further by opening a retail space and café with a clear mission: to place creativity at the core of everyday life. The retail space exudes a contemporary art gallery vibe, thanks to its ultra-minimalistic décor. The products on display are a carefully curated selection of ready-to-wear pieces and accessories, spread across the ground floor and basement.

It's hard to imagine a more contemporary setting, with its sleek minimalist design, ultra-healthy snacks and refreshments, and, most importantly, the meticulously selected range of men's and women's clothing.

Adjacent to the shop, the Gift Shop offers a thoughtful selection of books, records, stationery, and other unique items. Right next to it is a tiny but cosy café, run by Japanese coffee purveyors Dreamin' Man, serving expertly brewed coffee alongside healthy snacks and refreshments.

The Broken Arm is a playful homage to Marcel Duchamp's ready-made artwork, a snow shovel titled "In Advance of the Broken Arm."

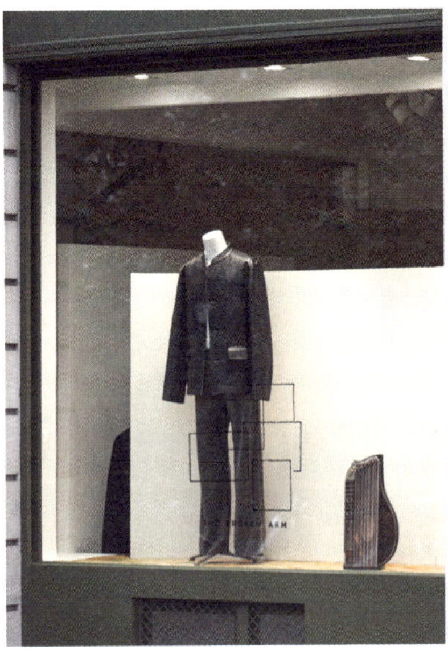

P.A.I.N.

YVON LAMBERT
LIBRAIRE ÉDITEU

Yvon Lambert Gallery

14 Rue des Filles Calvaire
75003 Paris

@librairieyvonlambert
yvon-lambert.com
+33 145 665584

Founded by visionary gallerist Yvon Lambert, this space in Paris's Marais district blends a bookshop, gallery, and publishing house into a unique cultural hub. Initially established in the 1960s as a gallery, Yvon Lambert was instrumental in introducing Europe to major figures of Conceptual, Minimal, and Land Art, including Cy Twombly, Sol LeWitt, and Lawrence Weiner, while championing European artists for over five decades.

In 2014, Lambert closed his gallery to focus on his passion for books and publishing. By 2017, alongside his daughter Ève, he inaugurated a new space at 14 Rue des Filles du Calvaire, designed by architect Dominique Perrault. This multifaceted venue continues Lambert's legacy, offering a meticulously curated selection of contemporary art books, rare editions, exhibition catalogues, and artist multiples. It also functions as a gallery space for exhibitions by both established and emerging artists and as a publishing house producing works on photography, literature, and limited-edition artist books.

THE NEXT DOOR

The Next Door

10 Rue Beaurepaire
75010 Paris

@thenextdoor
thenextdoor.fr
+33 142 001020

Once a must-visit in Avignon for the streetwear set, The Next Door brought its cult concept to Paris in 2019. Founder Nicolas Ivars, skate scene insider and street-style oracle, joined forces with Man/Woman fair founders Antoine Floch and Olivier Migda to create a next-level retail concept store. Located between Rue Yves Toudic and Rue Beaurepaire, the 800-square-metre space stretches across three levels with striking window façades that offer full views inside. The ground floor, anchored by ceiling-mounted racks, highlights pieces from the coolest French and international designer brands. Downstairs is streetwear heaven, with neon-lit sneakers from Nike, Adidas, Converse, and Asics lined up under black lights. There's even a sound-and-video art installation for the latest drop, think retail meets gallery. Upstairs, a serene lounge pairs vintage furniture with Bang & Olufsen sound systems, surrounded by a sharply curated collection of home objects and fashion. Don't forget to grab a coffee at Café Next Door. Yes, it's literally next door.

The Next Door is the next level concept store.

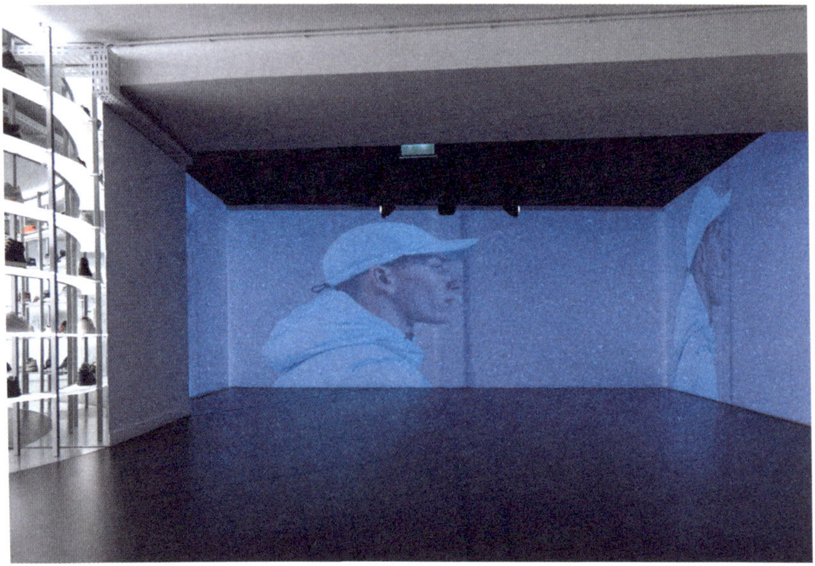

Words Sounds Colors & Shapes

1 rue Eugène Spuller
75003 Paris

@wordssoundscolorsandshapes
wordssoundscolorsandshapes.com

Words Sounds Colors & Shapes (formerly A Young Hiker) was founded in 2024 by multi-talented designer Ramdane Touhami. The name may have changed, but the concept remains: a unique store that reimagines the outdoor universe with razor-sharp style and zero clichés. Tucked near Jardin du Palais Royal, the space nods to Vieux Campeur, the legendary outfitter that has equipped French adventurers for over 80 years, but this is no ordinary gear shop. Think less hiking boots, more street-ready expedition.

Clothing and equipment are sourced directly from Japan and South Korea, reflecting Touhami's frequent travels and treks. With over 50 international brands, the store blends technical precision with a distinct Parisian edge, where function meets fashion without trying too hard. If the aesthetic resonates, the journey continues at Drei Berge, Touhami's mountain hotel in the Swiss Alps.

Words Sounds Colour & Shapes makes technical gear look almost glamorous, and might just tempt a mountain escape. Or at least a confident climb up the metro stairs.

DREI BERGE COLLECTION
Put your initials on your T-shirts and sweatshirts

EL CAPITAN

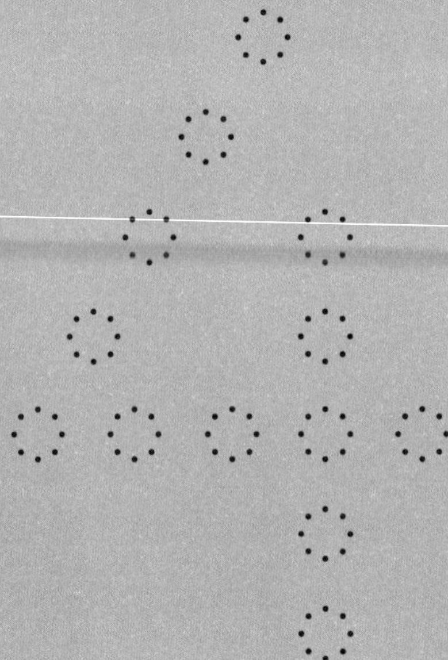

Amelie du Chalard Gallery
Bourse de Commerce
— The Pinault Collection
Fondation Cartier
Fondation Louis Vuitton
Galerie Patrick Seguin
Musée de l'Orangerie
Lafayette Anticipations
Musée National Picasso-Paris
Musée des Arts Décoratifs
Palais de Tokyo

Explore

Amelie du Chalard Gallery

18 Rue Séguier
75006 Paris

@amelieduchalard
amelieduchalard.com
+33 756 879068

Amelie du Chalard Gallery is housed in an 18th-century townhouse at 18 Rue Séguier, located between the Latin Quarter and Île de la Cité. Infused with a love of art and emotion, this exceptional 350m² space reflects the vision of gallery owner Amélie du Chalard.

Whether emerging or already represented in prestigious collections, Amélie du Chalard supports each artist whose common thread is their talent and the rare artistic methods that reveal the quality of their approach.

In 2015, Amélie du Chalard reimagined the traditional format of the contemporary art gallery. Visionary in her approach, she combined a commercial website with a house of art, where works adorn every wall. Close relationships with leading artists, as well as emerging talents, have allowed Amélie du Chalard to create an ecosystem around abstraction, comprising 200 artists who use diverse artistic genres: painting, sculpture, works on paper, photography, art objects, monumental installations, and site-specific works.

Where art lives not on white walls,
but in lived-in spaces.

Bourse de Commerce – The Pinault Collection

2 Rue de Viarmes
75001 Paris

@boursedecommerce
pinaultcollection.com
+33 155 046060

Housed in a striking 18th-century building, the Bourse de Commerce, Pinault Collection is a must-visit for art lovers and architects. Restored by renowned architect Tadao Ando, this former commodities exchange has been transformed into a dynamic cultural space showcasing the vast and thought-provoking collection of François Pinault.

The museum's circular design provides an immersive setting for rotating exhibitions that highlight some of the most influential artists of our time. From large-scale installations to intimate pieces, the collection spans a range of mediums, offering visitors a fresh perspective on the contemporary art scene. The restored frescoed dome and minimalist concrete additions create a stunning contrast between past and present, making the space as much a work of art as the pieces it houses.

Bourse de Commerce is Parisian poetry
in architectural form.

Fondation Cartier

261 Bd Raspail
75014 Paris

@fondationcartier
fondationcartier.com
+33 142 185650

For four decades, the Fondation Cartier pour l'art contemporain has been showcasing contemporary art, fostering creative freedom and bold artistic expression. Founded in 1984, it has continually provided a platform for established and emerging artists across disciplines, painting, photography, architecture, film, and design, encouraging experimentation and dialogue.

In 1994, the Fondation moved to Jean Nouvel's striking glass-and-steel building on Boulevard Raspail, a radical, open-space museum designed for flexibility and innovation. Now, as it embarks on a new chapter, the Fondation moves to the historic Place du Palais-Royal by the end of 2025. Set within a grand Haussmannian building, this new space, once the Grand Hôtel du Louvre and later the Louvre des Antiquaires, will again be transformed by Jean Nouvel, blending heritage with modernity.

With 8,500 m^2 of public space and adaptable exhibition areas, the new site will amplify the Fondation's mission of giving artists maximum creative freedom.

Fondation Louis Vuitton

8 Av. du Mahatma Gandhi
75116 Paris

@fondationlv
fondationlouisvuitton.fr
+33 140 699600

Rising like a ship unfurling its sails in the heart of the Bois de Boulogne, the Fondation Louis Vuitton is a true architectural pearl. Designed by visionary architect Frank Gehry, this extraordinary building defies convention with its billowing glass panels, 3,500 in total, curved and sculpted to capture light and movement. Beneath these shimmering sails, a structure of 19,000 concrete panels anchors the building, creating a striking balance between fluidity and solidity. There is hardly any other building that can be compared to this one. The project was initially presented in 2006, construction began in 2007 on a site in the Bois de Boulogne owned by the City of Paris, and it was finally completed in 2014.

First and foremost, this is a building designed to house modern art, unique in its architectural excellence. The collection features an ever-evolving selection of cutting-edge exhibitions, showcasing both established and emerging artists.

Looks like a spaceship, feels like a sculpture, functions as an art museum.

Galerie Patrick Seguin

5 Rue des Taillandiers
75011 Paris

@galeriepatrickseguin
patrickseguin.com
+33 147 003235

Established in 1989 by Patrick and Laurence Seguin, Galerie Patrick Seguin is situated in Paris's Bastille district within a 300 m^2 space designed by the acclaimed architect Jean Nouvel. The gallery has garnered international recognition for showcasing the works of prominent 20th-century French designers and architects, including Jean Prouvé, Charlotte Perriand, Pierre Jeanneret, Le Corbusier, and Jean Royère.

Renowned for its specialization in Jean Prouvé's creations, the gallery boasts an unparalleled collection of his demountable houses, innovative structures that are either unique or produced in limited quantities. This dedication has led to collaborations with esteemed institutions such as the Centre Georges Pompidou, the Museum of Modern Art in New York, and participation in events like the Venice Biennale. Beyond its curated exhibitions, Galerie Patrick Seguin actively engages in publishing monographs and catalogues that delve into the works of the designers it represents, enriching the discourse on 20th-century design.

Musée de l'Orangerie

Jardin des Tuileries
75001 Paris

@museeorangerie
musee-orangerie.fr
+33 144 504300

The Musée de l'Orangerie is located in the heart of Paris, within the Tuileries Garden, bordered by the Seine and overlooking Place de la Concorde. Its collections include *The Water Lilies*, the monumental masterpiece by Claude Monet, unveiled to the public when the museum opened in 1927. Displayed in two vast oval rooms, *The Water Lilies* represent the ambitious vision of a painter determined to capture every variation of light in his Giverny garden. Known worldwide, this masterpiece invites endless contemplation.

In the 1960s, the Musée de l'Orangerie became home to the *Arts à Paris* collection, featuring works by Renoir, Cézanne, Matisse, Picasso, Modigliani, Rousseau, and Soutine. This collection reflects the artistic vibrancy of the late 19th and early 20th centuries, showcasing a period of extraordinary creative innovation.

Lafayette Anticipations

9 Rue du Plâtre
75004 Paris

@lafayetteanticipations
lafayetteanticipations.com
+33 142 828998

In 2018 The Fondation d'entreprise Galeries Lafayette opened its doors to the public in an industrial building renovated by architect Rem Koolhaas. As a space for exhibiting and creating art, Lafayette Anticipations is a laboratory for creativity, innovation and research that is open to all members of the public. Located in the heart of Paris in the Marais district, Lafayette Anticipations invites visitors to discover other ways of seeing, feeling, and listening to today's world to better imagine, thanks to artists, the world of tomorrow.

At the core of the building is a striking exhibition tower, featuring two sets of mobile platforms that can be rearranged to create ever-changing spatial configurations. The ground floor serves as an open agora, a space for gathering and exchanging ideas. Free and open to the public, visitors can explore exhibitions, browse the carefully curated selection at La Librairie, or enjoy a meal at Pluto, the café-restaurant led by chef Thomas Coupeau, offering a menu that evolves from day to night.

This isn't just a gallery, it's a shape-shifting art lab with a Rem Koolhaas soul.

LAFAYETTE
Fondation
d'entreprise
Galeries
Lafayette
ANTICIPATIONS

Musée National Picasso-Paris

5 Rue de Thorigny
75003 Paris

@museepicassoparis
museepicassoparis.fr
+33 185 560036

The Musée Picasso Paris holds an extraordinary collection of over 5,000 works and more than 200,000 archival items. With its remarkable scope and variety, it is the only public collection in the world that offers a comprehensive view of Picasso's artistic evolution, spanning painting, sculpture, engraving, and drawing, while also providing insight into his creative process.

On 12 March 2024, the museum unveiled a new, three-storey presentation of its collection, marking ten years since its grand reopening. Now permanently housed in the historic Hôtel Salé, the display unfolds across 22 rooms, bringing together nearly 400 pieces, including paintings, sculptures, ceramics, drawings, and prints from every phase of Picasso's career.

This permanent exhibition follows a year of celebrations dedicated to Picasso, which encouraged reflection and dialogue around his legacy. With this reimagined display and an engaging programme of events, the Musée National Picasso-Paris invites visitors to continuously explore, question, and appreciate the depth and complexity of the artist's work.

Three storeys, 400 works, and a lifetime of reinvention. Picasso didn't stick to one style, why should the museum?

Musée des Arts Décoratifs

107 Rue de Rivoli
75001 Paris

@madparis
madparis.fr
+33 144 555750

The Musée des Arts Décoratifs (MAD), located inside the Louvre's west wing, is a sanctuary for design and history lovers. Bridging the worlds of art and craftsmanship, it has showcased centuries of creative ingenuity since taking up residence in the Pavillon de Marsan in 1905. Today, it holds one of the world's most remarkable collections of decorative arts.

Spanning from the Middle Ages to today, MAD's collection is a deep dive into the evolution of style, design, and function. Its galleries take visitors on a journey through time, with rooms dedicated to different eras of French history, from opulent 18th-century salons to sleek Art Deco interiors. Thematic displays highlight everything from exquisite glassware and jewellery to lavish furniture and fashion. So whether you're fascinated by centuries-old craftsmanship or cutting-edge contemporary design, MAD offers a captivating look at how beauty and utility have shaped our world.

L'INCOERENZA È UN RISULTATO STRAORDINARIO
E LIKE FIRE LIKE REVOLUTION IO DI M
AROT

Palais de Tokyo

13 Av. du Président Wilson
75116 Paris

@palaisdetokyo
palaisdetokyo.com/
+33 181 97 35 88

One of the most exciting museums in Paris and a top destination in Europe for contemporary and modern art, Palais de Tokyo has been a game-changer since its creation in 2002. With its dynamic, playful, and boundary-pushing approach, it redefined the city's relationship with contemporary art. More than just a museum, it stands as a rebellious, ever-evolving space in the 16th arrondissement, an unconventional yet ambitious "palace" of creativity, exchange, and surprise.

Its influence extends well beyond France, inspiring institutions and art lovers alike with its bold programming. In 2012, Palais de Tokyo underwent a major transformation, expanding from 8,000 to 22,000 square meters, making it one of the largest centres for contemporary creativity in Europe. Stretching to the banks of the Seine, it now forms a vibrant link between the Eiffel Tower and the Champs-Élysées, a true hub where art, culture, and innovation collide.

Not your grandma's museum.
Palais de Tokyo plays by no rules but its own.

Index

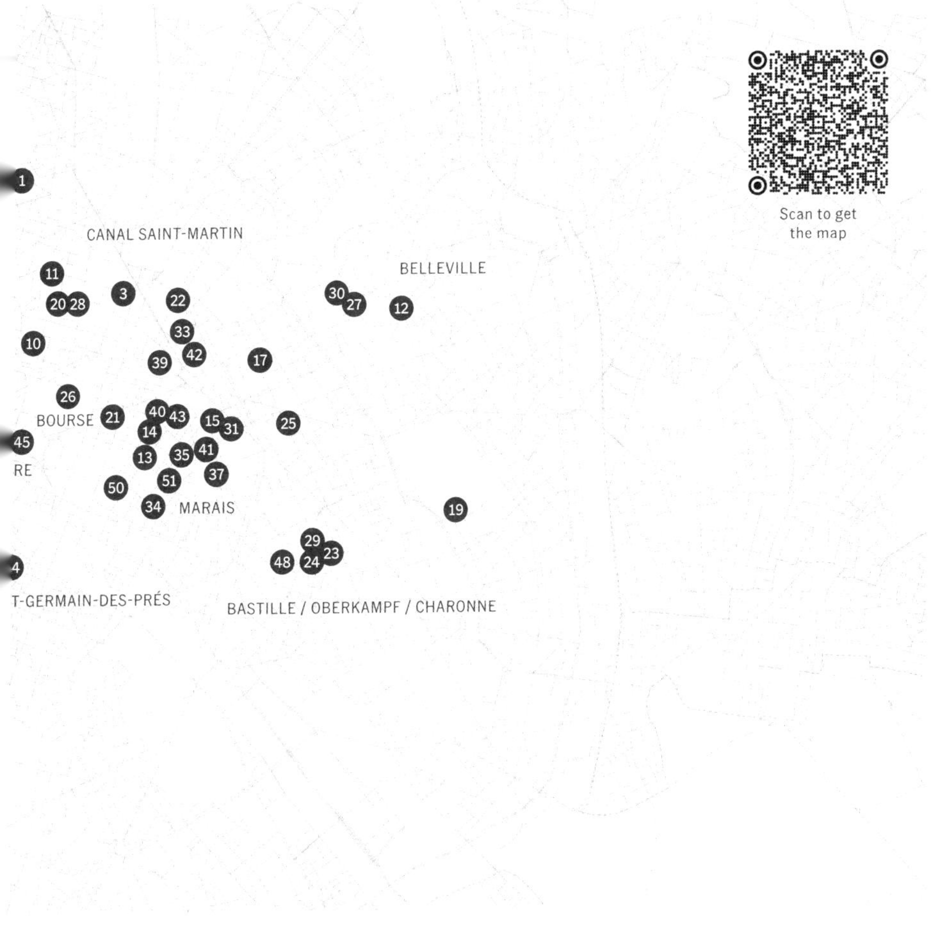

Scan to get the map

Mads Arlien-Søborg is a Copenhagen-based journalist and lifestyle expert. He holds a master's degree in modern Culture and Communication from University of Copenhagen. Mads has worked with design, fashion and lifestyles for many years. He has hosted several television shows about travel, design and architecture.

New Mags is more than a bookstore; it's a destination where art and literature converge, offering a select array of lifestyle books, magazines, and accessories. Founded in 2016 in Horsens, Jutland by Jesper Svangård and Jesper Oxholm Mikkelsen. Their dream of a space that not only stores but celebrates books culminated in the opening of their first showroom in Copenhagen in 2021.

NOTES

NOTES

NOTES

Front cover:
© Mads Arlien-Soeborg

Destination:
© Unsplash / @KevinWeil / BenoitLinero / Pixelmeister / The Social Food Studio / Pexels / PasillasLimber / MatthieuGouiffes

Neighbourhoods:
© BenoitLinero / Pexels / Unsplash / @unburattinoqualunque

Stay:
Élysée Montmartre: Courtesy of Élysée Montmartre
Hotel Amour: © PionPhotographie
Hotel Grand Amour: © PionPhotographie / Pionstudio
Grand Pigalle Experimental: © Mr. Tripper
L'Eldorado: © BenoitLinero
Hotel Piscine Molitor: Courtesy of Hotel Piscine Molitor
Hôtel des Académies et des Arts: © BenoitLinero
Le Grand Hôtel Cayré: © Gilbert Kann
Le Pigalle: © BenoitLinero
The Hoxton Paris: Courtesy of The Hoxton

Taste:
Amagat: Courtesy of Amagat
Aux Deux Amis: © Yuto Fujimoto
Café Pigalle: Courtesy of Café Pigalle
Café Shin: © Jules Focone
Candle Kids Coffee: © Matteo Verzini
Chez Georges: © The Social Food Studio
Clamato: © Mickaël A. Bandassak / Maurine Toussaint
Combat: © Christophe Meireis
Delicatessen Cave: Courtesy of Delicatessen Cave
Derrière: © Constance Dero
Deviant: Courtesy of Deviant
Dreamin' Man: Courtesy of Dreamin' Man
Early June: © Lucia Bell Epstein
Halo: Courtesy of Halo
La Baratin: Courtesy of Baratin
Le Chateaubriand: Courtesy of Le Chateaubriand
Recto Verso: Courtesy of Recto Verso
Septime: © Maurine Toussaint / F. Flohic / Mickaël A. Bandassak
Septime La Cave: © Maurine Toussaint / Mickaël A. Bandassak
Sevenly Heart: Courtesy of Sevenly Heart
Union Boulangerie: Courtesy of Union Boulangerie

Shop:
Arrogant Verneuil: Courtesy of Arrogant Verneuil
Centre Commercial: Courtesy of Centre Commercial
Dover Street Market: © Maurits Peeters
Jimmy Fairly: Courtesy of Jimmy Fairly
Le Bon Marché: Courtesy of Le Bon Marché
Merci #1: Courtesy of Merci
Merci #2: © Tempe Storm Cole
Saint Laurent Babylone: Courtesy of Saint Laurent
Thanx God I'm a VIP: Courtesy of Thanx God I'm a VIP
The Broken Arm: © Quentin Randrianarivelo
Yvon Lambert Gallery: Courtesy of Yvon Lambert Gallery
Words Sounds Colors & Shapes: © Quentin Lacombe
The Next Door: Courtesy of The Next Door

Explore:
Amelie Maison D'art: Courtesy of Amelie du Chalard Gallery
Bourse de Commerse: © Marc Domage / Maxime Tétard / Patrick Tourneboeuf
Fondation Cartier: © Luc Boegly / Jean Nouvel
Fondation Louis Vuitton: © Iwan Baan
Galerie Patrick Seguin: © Galerie Patrick Seguin
Lafayette Anticipations: © Marc Domage / Chloé Magdelaine / Delfino Sisto Legnani / Marco Cappelletti
Musée de l'Orangerie: © Sophie Crépy
Musée national Picasso: © Musée national Picasso-Paris, Béatrice Hatala / Musée national Picasso-Paris, Voyez-Vous, Chloé Vollmer / Musée national Picasso-Paris
Musée des Arts Décoratifs: © Philippe Chancel / Laszlo Horvath
Palais de Tokyo: © Aurélien Mole / Florent Michel / 11h45 / Aurélien Mole

NEW MAGS CITY GUIDE
PARIS

Editor-In-Chief: Mads Arlien-Søborg
Publisher: New Mags
Sales: Jesper Svangård, New Mags

Art Direction: Studio8585
Design Director: Mario Depicolzuane
Design & Layout: Benja Pavlin, Varshini KVSS

ISBN: 97887-85374-10-3

MIX
Paper | Supporting responsible forestry
FSC® C129413
FSC www.fsc.org

2nd Edition 2026
Printed at Print Best, Estonia, 2026

Published in 2026 by New Mags
& Helmin Publishing

New Mags city guides are available at special discounts when purchased in quantity for premiums and promotions as well as fundraising or educational use. For details, contact post@new-mags.com or the address below.

Buy the Books Online: new-mags.com

New Mags, Office & Distribution
Vejlevej 13, 8700 Horsens, Denmark
new-mags.com

NEW MAGS

Helmin Publishing
Nivå Strandpark 21, 1, 2990 Nivå, Denmark
helminpublishing.dk

This book contains a curated selection of the editor's favourite places and should be used for its intended purpose, as a guide. It is by no means comprehensive of all the amazing locations the city has to offer. Since changes may have occurred since publication, we recommend using the contact information for each location to ensure up-to-date details.

The editor and publisher wish to express their gratitude to everyone who played a role in making this book possible: the staff, friends and families, brands, and organizations. A big thank you to Fujifilm® for giving us the opportunity to create beautiful city images for the book.